I0480462

THE RETAIL INVESTOR

How to Achieve Financial Freedom through Passive Investing, Real Estate and Online Businesses

Big Jodhi

Book cover illustrated by Kristen Kiong

ASIN: B08FZGD69V

Cover design by: Kristen Kiong
Printed in the United States of America

CONTENTS

INTRODUCTION

Welcome back my fellow capitalist pigs. It's time to put whatever you have learnt in the previous book into practice! What if I told you that you would only need around $230,000 to be financially secured for life? Investing is an extremely fun process, but more importantly, it must have some meaning, to you, the investor, at least. If not, why invest at all? The money that you gain must be put to some meaningful use.

Let's address the why. The why of investing. For a typical person, the term financial freedom means that one does not have to think about money every again; to go on trips whenever one wants, to look at the left side of the menu instead of the right (where the price of this dish is usually quoted), to be able to help out a family member in need of financial aid, to give to charities, to have the *freedom of choice*. Money gives you choices, and this book is your path to freedom, financial freedom that is.

We'll also discuss several other ways we can earn income aside from your regular day job. So grab a cup o' Joe, sit back, relax, and let this 2nd part of "The Retail Investor" take you on a ride, a ride towards your financial freedom.

CHAPTER 1

Getting the Inspiration.

P icture this. Imagine that you have enough money till the day you meet your maker. You have no worries, no obligations (aside from family), nothing. What would a typical day be like for you? Let me give you an example.

7am – Wake up.

715am – Send kids to school.

8am – Back home. Start a morning run.

830am – Freshen up.

845am – Laundry.

9am – Breakfast and watching the morning news/ reading.

1020am – go for a movie, on your own or with your husband or wife.

1pm – Pick up kids from school.

130pm – Kids freshen up, start homework.

3pm – Kids done with homework, off to playground, shopping malls, zoo, arcade etc.

6pm – Dinner.

7pm – Quality time with family.

10pm – Bedtime.

Let's call this activity "The Freedom Exercise". Now, using this template, I would like you to personalise it. Relate it back to you. Replace it with activities that you would do when you are free of work, and of course, free of the stress of needing to earn money. Look at the list, close your eyes and envision yourself going through the activities of the day. How does it feel?

Feels great doesn't it? Without a care in the world, you do what you like, when you like. No stress, no obligation to wake up early, no frustrating morning commutes, no lunchtime crowds, no demanding bosses, no deadlines, no unhappy clients to service, nothing. Just you, and the choices that you decide to make for yourself. You do what you want to do. You are no longer a slave to money because you have enough of it! You do not have to slog it out day in day out, enduring all kinds of displeasures because you simply have no choice (unless you are ok with starving).

Now, if this exercise has stirred your soul, and you honestly desire to have a life like this, then good for you! Let me tell you that this is possible. In fact, it's not just possible, it's an absolute certainty if you would just follow what this book says. If you want this so bad that you can taste it, even better, you WILL achieve it. What is this visceral feeling that you feel? It's desire. To be a little more specific, it's burning desire. And let me tell you my fellow capitalist pig, this is the first step towards financial freedom. You get inspired to achieve what you desire. Do yourself a favour, print out a copy of your "Freedom Exercise" and paste it in your bedroom somewhere. Make sure you read it every morning.

When you have a burning desire to achieve something, you will eventually achieve it. It just reshapes your whole outlook on life and what your purpose is.

Do you often feel that there is more to life than what you're currently doing? Most of us have routine jobs. We work without knowing why we work. We have herd mentality. My friends and family work, so, I work. Get out of that mindset. Find your purpose. Find your passion. If your passion is art, fill your freedom exercise with art activities. If your passion is underprivileged kids, fill it up with visits to orphanages. Heck, if your passion is freaking playing world of warcraft, fill it with 40-man instance raids from 7am to 7am (the next day). I don't care, as long as the thought of whatever you have on your freedom exercise gets you excited!

I'm not saying that the path to contentment is to stop

working, if you love your job, by all means, continue working even after you have achieved financial freedom. The crux of the matter is, most people are not inspired by what they can achieve with money, hence they do not observe the rules of money that will inevitably get them stinking rich. To quote Dave Ramsay, getting rich is 20% mechanics and 80% behaviour. Your psychology, making wise decisions with your spending, saving, and investing, it all plays a huge part in making your ideal lifestyle come true. So what I am saying is, get a dream, a goal, an ambition of some sort, really feel it in your bones, and be disciplined on taking the steps to achieve it.

CHAPTER 2

The Money Champion.

S omeone told me a while back, "Big Jo, don't be so hard up about money, it can be earned back." This phrase stuck with me for a while. Can we really look at money that way? I knew I heard this phrase multiple times before, and it sickens me to know that hogwash like this is being passed on to people, and worse still, to generations after us.

You see, anyone who says this, obviously does not understand how precious money is, the blood, sweat and tears that is required when earning it, and the power that money gives its owner when put in the right place. People who utter this phrase are not champions of money, hence they don't have it. Money must be treated as precious, if not it will slip from your grasp.

So, how do we become money champions? First and foremost, Work. Find work and earn money. Aim to earn lots of it. Don't squander it though, every cent that you earn must have a destination. Ask yourself this; do you often feel that you have more "month" at the end of the "money" (your monthly wages that is)? Because you're not keeping tracking of where your money is going! Have a budget, so that you know how much you're spending, and ultimately, how much you're saving. If you don't tell your money where to go, it'll go wherever it wants to go, out of your bank account.

Next, be a business owner, not a consumer. What do I mean by this? People know Apple; they buy their products, queue up for long hours at their outlets for the latest iPhones. But chances are, none of these blokes ever thought of owning a share of Apple. In order to be a money champion, you must adopt the mind of a business owner. Use your savings to invest. Get into the stock market game. The stock market is the single greatest vehicle for all retail investors to get rich! And people are afraid of it (go figure). Stocks give the BEST returns compared to other investment classes (bonds, real estate, commodities etc.) I stress again, ignorance is poverty, and people are afraid of the stock market because they are ignorant, they do not take time to learn about it and get their feet wet into the game of investing. Instead, they choose to take the route of the consumer and buy a home (with a huge mortgage of course), a big TV and a car instead.

Poverty-minded people are consumers who love to buy things that do not generate cashflow. They accumulate useless items, or even worse, liabilities. They don't buy assets. Money champions accumulate assets that generate cashflow. Be a business owner, not a consumer.

Lastly, practice giving. Give to charities, support your religious beliefs, fund a college education for a child in a low-income family, build schools in Africa, upgrade your local libraries. Do something to benefit the people around you. When you can accumulate money, learn to give it away eventually. When the steel tycoon Andrew Carnegie died, they discovered a sheet of paper upon which he had written one of the major goals of his life; he aimed to spend the first half of his life accumulating money and to spend the last half of his life giving it all away. What a character. As money champions, we must understand that we are actually stewards of the money that we have been blessed with, and the right thing to do is to give, at least a portion of it away at some point. The single greatest joy that a human being can experience is giving, being outrageously generous to others will make you feel like a real champion. Practice giving.

CHAPTER 3

Work. Hard. Don't take your income for granted!

P eople love to complain about their jobs. They hate the pay. They hate the work hours. Colleagues. Bosses. Customers. Everything about their day is bad. It's really funny how people complain about being paid too little, when chances are, the value that they bring to their own workplace is mediocre at best. It's like talking to a fireplace on a cold day, "ok fire please start on your own first, when you're big enough and producing enough heat, then I'll add the wood." Seriously? Is this the mentality of our affluent middle class today? Ok my apologies, I tend to get a little cynical with people who are negative about their jobs, but honestly I just can't comprehend why people would take their jobs for granted, especially when it's their job that gives them the ability to live. it's so strange that people complain about the one thing that actually feeds them, provides for their children, entertainment, and a roof over their heads. If you are one of those that hate your job, ask yourself this: would you rather be on the streets, starving, begging? Having a job, is the single best thing that any human being can have. A job gives you a form of social standing and brand about yourself, and it keeps you busy, while making you money at the same time. Then why do people often hate their jobs? It boils down to the same issue discussed in the previous chapter, inspiration. Motivation towards a worthwhile goal.

So, there are many reasons why people dislike their jobs. It can be the nature of work, handling unreasonable customers, toxic work environment, demanding bosses, or a supposedly meagre compensation. Two ways you can solve this for yourself.

Solution 1. Leave the darn job. It actually speaks more about your own insecurity and self-worth when you stick to a job that you hate, because you are the one contributing to all the negativity not only in your mind, but to others as well. Consider what is a deal breaker for you to leave your job. Write down a list of things that you like about your job, and a list of things that you hate about your job. If you find that there are issues that really just make you sick, make a firm decision to leave it, and search for something better. Be wise about it though, you're risking your entire livelihood on this decision. Make sure you have a backup plan.

Solution 2. Change your mindset and perspective about your job. Similar to the first solution, do up a list of likes and dislikes about your current job. Find out the things that motivate you about your job. Be thankful for those positive pointers. And, for things that you are unhappy about, find ways to shift your mindset to look at these negative pointers in a different light, or better still, find solutions to turn the negative pointers into not so negative ones. For instance, if your department is particularly toxic, you can avoid the toxic co-workers or request a shift to another department. If your customers are unreasonable, find ways to go out of your way to service them, satisfy them, and amaze them with your customer service. You'd be surprised how an unhappy customer can be turned into your greatest fan. If you have demanding superiors, try and understand that they have deadlines and requirements that they're trying to fulfil. Ask yourself this question: what is my superior's KPI/ goal/ objective and how do I help him or her achieve it? Or how do I make my superior's job easier? To help him or her worry less about the department. Pivot your behaviours, actions and thinking towards this angle and you will almost certainly have a much easier time with your superiors. Easier said than done though, then again, nothing worthwhile doing comes easy.

To put things plainly, if you would just put in 110% effort in everything you do at work (easier said than done, I get it, but you have to put in the effort if you want to enjoy the good things in life), serving your clients, customers, and superiors, you will have a much easier time at work. Why? Because you are bringing value to people around you. When you get recognised for being a person that adds value to anyone you're interacting with, you will receive social, and financial recognition; your pay will be directly correlated to the value that you bring to the table. You'd naturally feel better about yourself and your work as well.

Don't wish for things to get easier, instead, wish that you become better at what you do, increase your capacity, and things will get easier in the long run. Don't be lazy about work. Even the simplest job will bring in money, and remember, with every dime you collect and save, you can potentially bring in more nickels and dimes through investing (more of this in our later chapters). Never look down on any kind of work. And never, ever, take your existing job for granted. Work your tail off. Nothing beats the satisfaction of a hard day of fulfilling work.

CHAPTER 4

Save. As much you can!

D o you find yourself being constantly out of money before the month ends? How does that make you feel?

I remembered when I was in my 20s, still living with my parents, I would spend my months' wages in 2 weeks, and then going to my mum for extra money. It made me feel lousy because I felt so dependent and irresponsible, and I was irresponsible. The feeling of not having money is horrible. I eventually decided to change my ways and became more disciplined in saving. It has done wonders. I feel happier about myself and I don't feel the guilt that I used to feel for being so loose with my wages.

One problem that I faced was not knowing where my money went, it just seemed to disappear without me knowing. So, as I listened to Dave Ramsay (please Google him if you don't know who I'm talking about, this man is a personal finance guru), he said that everyone MUST have a written budget, and stick to it. Now, budgets are tough to maintain, chances are, we would not follow the budgets that we create. So maybe, let's take a baby step 0.5, instead of the usual baby steps from the Financial Peace University. Instead of doing a Budget, start by tracking all your expenses first. Track them for a month. Every single penny. At the end of the month, go through your list of expenses and you'll have a revelation on how much money you're actually wasting, whether it's on five dollar lattes from Starbucks, or a subscription service that you hardly use, like a gym membership or Netflix. Then slowly start cutting from there. Take note of the total amount of expenses that you cut, and with that, add a final expense, title it "pay yourself first." That's the tax that you're going to put on your total salary for the month. This is the way to get rich. A part of all you earn is yours to keep. Save, and the next chapter will show you how you can invest your way to financial freedom later, using the savings that you have accumulated. I use an app called Wally to track my expenses, it's really useful, I'd recommend downloading that app on your smart phone for tracking expenses.

It's definitely a sacrifice to reduce your standard of living, at least for a while. I understand. It's tough to let go of all these luxuries. It's just too painful and demoralising, living below your means. If you really can't bring yourself to cutting down your expenses, my only advice is, to work hard at your job and increase your value there. Otherwise, getting financially secure is really just a pipe dream for you. Nothing worth doing comes easy. And if you're willing to make the sacrifice, you'll enjoy the fruits of your labour in time to come.

CHAPTER 5

The Freedom Fund.

The term "financial freedom" gets thrown around a lot. I won't be surprised if it actually scares some people. This absolute number that is so big that most of us think it's unattainable. What do you think that number is? 1 million? 2 million? Suze Orman says the number is 10 million dollars, to retire comfortably. No wonder people are giving up and spending like children. Let me give you some hope. It's not. In fact, it's way smaller than you think it actually is. With the right strategy and mindset, you too can reach a basic level of financial freedom, most of the time, way before official retirement age.

Let's analyse the two words "financial freedom". It literally means free from financial obligations. So, in your own life, what are your financial obligations? I'm talking about needs here, not wants. Let's break it down and list the order of importance. 1 being the most important of course.

1. Mortgage/rent
2. Food and water
3. Utilities
4. Transportation
5. Insurance

These are your 5 main expenses that you need to cover to at least live decently. So, if you can find a way to generate enough income passively (we'll explain this in our later chapters) that can cover all the 5 main expenses, then technically, you are financially secure! So first things first, let's figure out those monthly expense numbers. Use your Wally app to help you with this. I'll use my own personal expenses as an example.

1. Mortgage/rent - $1,200
2. Food and water - $500
3. Utilities - $100
4. Transportation - $140
5. Insurance - $60

Add those expenses up and you get a whopping $2,000 a month in basic expenditure. $24,000 a year.

Now, we need a freedom fund. This fund will buy you out of slavery, slavery from financial obligations that is. This is the total amount of capital that you must accumulate, through savings and investments, that would allow you to yield a passive income of $24,000 annually, without having you physically working for it. Before I forget, let me share that there are 3 main types of income:

Active income – any type of income that requires your time, presence, availability, and energy. This is usually your job. You are trading time for money. This is the worst type of income to rely on.

Portfolio income – any type of income that comes from investments. Dividends and capital gains are some examples of portfolio income.

Passive income – any type of income that does not require you managing it. The income flows to you automatically. An example would be a private business that you have built up and others are running the business for you. You're not required to manage it and still get income from it.

Ok, good that we got that out of the way. This book mainly talks about portfolio income, and a little bit of passive income as well, but we'll come to that later. First, please think about your yearly expenses number ready before reading the next paragraph.

The great motivational speaker and financial guru Tony Robbins explains the freedom fund concept very clearly in one of his YouTube videos; search for "Tony Robbins tap the power", his video should pop up. I would also highly recommend anyone to get a copy of two of his books "Money: master the game" and "unshakeable". these two books changed my life (apart from rich dad poor dad).

According to Tony Robbins, there are 3 levels of financial freedom:

Financial security - this first stage is where basic necessities are covered. Passive income from your freedom fund covers basic expenses.

Financial independence - this second stage includes having everything else covered. A good benchmark for this is when your passive income is the same as your salary.

Financial freedom - this is the final stage, where you literally can't outspend your freedom fund. Everything you can think of is covered by your passive income.

Sounds awesome doesn't it? I hope you're motivated by this. Let's not get over the top here, we'll first set a goal to hit level 1, which is financial security. $24,000 is my number, I hope you have yours. Let's go on to the next chapter to see how we can achieve this.

CHAPTER 6

Invest in the Stock Market.

T he stock market is the single most effective vehicle to grow your wealth safely and steadily. In my previous book, "The Retail Investor: How to Analyse Businesses in the Stock Market", I go into the nitty gritty of analysing financial statements and how to make practical stock purchases. Do yourselves a favour and grab a copy of it too.

Anyway, back to the stock market. Contrary to popular belief, the stock market is actually NOT risky. However, you must have these 3 requirements.

Holding power

Have holding power for your stock market investments. The stock market has returned on average between 8~10% in total investment returns historically. This percentage, however, is averaged out through 50 to 70 years. Some years it can earn as much as 30% and some years it can go down as much as 90% (read up on stock market performance during the Great Depression in the 1930s). When deciding on how much of your savings you want in the stock market, always consider funds that you know for sure that you won't need to use for at least the next 5-10 years. You don't want to be caught "Swimming naked in the sea when the tide goes out", having to liquidate your portfolio of stock market investments during a recession or a bear market season. Stocks are super volatile in the short term but we always know where the stock market goes in the long term, it goes up. Why? Because of human potential, productivity, innovation and of course an increase in population as well. Human beings need goods and service to live, what are the chances that 10-15 years from now the global economic machine will produce less than today? Unless of course a comet hits the earth, or an all-out nuclear war. When that happens, I think your best investment would be buying an eBook on how to hunt for food effectively.

Diversify

Tell me something. Is it logical to put all your savings into a single company? There was once a hand phone company, called Nokia. When I was in school, every kid owned at least a Nokia 3310 (those bulky handphones that could stop a bus). They were very clearly the dominant players in the mobile phone industry. At their peak, they probably earned about 4 billion in profits. Where are they now? Acquired by Microsoft. Sad. From being the dominant mobile phone company, to losing their market value from a high of about 25 euros per share in 2007 to less than 2 euros in 2013. A 92% decline in value. Imagine if you were to dump all your savings of say $50,000 in your the "sure win" investment, Nokia, you would have lost $46,000, with no recovery in sight. So, when you purchase stocks, always make sure you do your research, and buy at least 8-10 companies if you're confident. Alternatively, just index. I'll explain more on this later in the chapter.

No such thing as get rich quick

If you have a gambler's mentality to get rich quick, stay out of the stock market. Your greed and lack of knowledge will lead you to make dumb purchases based on seemingly hot (actually scammy) stock tips. If there's one thing to understand about the laws of wealth, it is that to attain a lot of wealth, you must have a rich mindset (money champion), and money champions with the rich mindset know that getting rich quick is a myth. Legendary motivational speaker Jim Rohn once said that if you take all the money in the world, divide it up equally among everybody, eventually the money will still end up back in the same pockets. Why is this so? Because every individual has a certain wealth mindset. If you have a rich mindset, you'll be rich. If you have a poverty mindset, no matter how much money you get your hands on, you're bound to lose all of it eventually. There are countless cases of celebrities, Star Athletes, lottery winners who hit it big time and make a ton of money at one point of their lives, only to lose it all eventually. Johnny Depp, Francis Ford Coppola, Mike Tyson, just to name a few. Getting rich quick does not exist, don't think that a stock will shoot up 1000% within a few days. Don't gamble. And for goodness sake, don't get me started on bitcoin.

Alright sorry for the sermon. I digress. Back to investing.

As you all know, I'm a major proponent of the stock market investing. Whether or not you pick individual stocks, mutual funds, or ETFs, doesn't really matter, as Long as you get into the game of stock market investing. Now here's another concept that needs no introduction: compound interest.

Let me tell you the story of two friends, William and James. William starts investing at 23, the age that he starts working. He puts away $500 dollars a month ($6,000 annually) and does this for 10 years, stops at 33, and just leaves it in the stock market to grow (8% compounded). The table below shows how much he accumulated over the years till he hits 65.

William	
Age	**Freedom Fund**
23	6,000
24	12,480
25	19,478
26	27,037
27	35,200
28	44,016
29	53,537
30	63,820
31	74,925
32	86,919
33	93,873
65	**1,101,794**

James does the exact same thing, but he starts at age 35 instead, and he continues to save and invest all the way till he reaches 65. Let's see how much he has at 65.

James			
Age	Freedom Fund	Age	Freedom Fund
35	6,000	51	202,501
36	12,480	52	224,701
37	19,478	53	248,678
38	27,037	54	274,572
39	35,200	55	302,538
40	44,016	56	332,741
41	53,537	57	365,360
42	63,820	58	400,589
43	74,925	59	438,636
44	86,919	60	479,726
45	99,873	61	524,105
46	113,863	62	572,033
47	128,972	63	623,796
48	145,290	64	679,699
49	162,913	65	**740,075**
50	181,946		

As seen in both tables, not only did William accumulate substantially more money than James ($361,000 more to be exact, almost 50% more), but he also did it with less capital. William saved a grand total of $6000 x 10 years = $60,000, while James saved a grand total of $6000 x 30 years = $180,000. So let's sum up, William puts in less money than James and still has more than his friend when he retires at 65! The critical difference was starting earlier! Time is the most important element in compound interest.

So let's look back at our own expense numbers, shall we? We know how much we earn per month, we know how much we spend, which leads to knowing how much we save. We know our number for financial security, we know how compounding interest works. Let's discuss the type of stock investment vehicle we can put our monthly savings in.

Typically, the simplest method is to automate your savings to buy an index fund. Preferably from the country that you live in, if you're a US citizen, S&P 500 or DJIA index fund or ETF will do the trick, if you're English, it's footsie. If you're Aussie, ASX. An index fund or a market index ETF buys the top companies in the countries of your choosing, and they bundle it up to make it a single stock; you save money on the brokers fees, management fees and you get diversification. In addition, market indices beat most fund managers who pick stocks. In other words, for all the quants and hedge fund managers out there who charge ludicrous fees for their "investment expertise", they actually don't beat a simple index fund or an index ETF over the long term, so, indexing is the way to go.

Now, there are two methods that you can pay for your financial security stage using your freedom fund. The first method to is to slowly sell off a piece of the freedom fund annually, so that you have liquidity for your expenses. Typically, a recommended amount would be 4 percent annually. The good thing about this method is that you don't have to save as much money compared to the 2nd method which I'm going to share with you shortly. The downside of the first method is that you slowly eat away into your principal, which means you have to really plan and watch your budget properly, to ensure that you have cash flow for as long as you live.

So how big must my freedom fund be for method 1?

25 x $24,000 = $600,000.

This method is called FIRE (Financial independence retire early). The FIRE concept emphasises on aggressive savings. So, according to FIRE, if you can save 75% of your income, you can technically be financially secure in less than 10 years. If you're 30 and reading this, it means that you can be financially secure by 40!

The second method is to live off the dividends of your freedom fund. Typically, index funds give about 2-3 percent in dividends annually, so your freedom fund number must actually be around 30 to 50 times your annual expenses, compared to the first method where you only need say around 25 times your annual expenses. Let's use my personal expenses number of $24,000 again.

If my investments yield 2% in dividends, the freedom fund would be 50 x $24,000 = $1.2 million.

If my investments yield 3% in dividends, the freedom fund would be 30 x $24,000 = $720,000.

Similar to FIRE, a high savings rate will fast track your financial goals. Obviously.

Now, the second method may seem daunting, but re-member that companies grow in profits, and dividends will likely increase as the years go by. If you can, put aside as much money as you can into investing, espe-cially if you're still in your twenties, it will be the best decision of your life. Go for the 2nd method of invest-ing, yes, it'll take longer, but it'll also last a lot longer as your principal amount/ freedom fund is left totally untouched.

CHAPTER 7

Other forms of income.

Now that we know what our freedom fund number is, being financially secure doesn't seem that impossible now does it? It is relatively far away, I'm sure most of us will take at least 10-12 years. But at the very least there is light at the end of the tunnel.

For those of you weird people who are even more determined to reach your financial objectives faster, there are only 2 options: reduce your expenses, or earn more money. Plain and simple. The best profession to increase income quickly is a salesperson, the sky is the limit for the salesperson if he or she is effective. If you're in a sales job, I hope that this book gives you the motivation and hunger that you need to close more deals. For those of us with fixed wages, do not fear. There are avenues that we can increase our income, other than through our job promotions. Here are some practical ways to give a boost to your income.

The Internet

The internet age has given us the opportunity to make untold amounts of money. Just Google Ryan Kaji. He is the highest paid kid YouTube Star, generating $22 million dollars in 2018. What does he do on his YouTube channel Ryan Toysreview? His dad simply films him playing and unboxing toys! Sounds simple? Certainly. Ryan had 17 million followers in 2018. The power of the internet has allowed so much influence and connectivity globally, that starting online businesses become so simple to start and lucrative at the same time.

YouTube

YouTube is a great platform for earning side income. Think of it as sort of a tv station, run by a single person, the youtuber. The image of the channel, video content, filming, editing, and posting can all be done by a single person. A YouTuber would set up a channel, post interesting videos on his or her channel, attract as many viewers as possible and hopefully convert them to subscribers. Then, when the channel grows to at least 1000 subscribers, with 4000 hours of watch time within the span on a year, the channel can be monetized by YouTube. This means that, because the channel has a good chunk a regular viewers, it would worthwhile for YouTube to place ads on the videos posted by that channel. The value of a channel is largely dependent on the number of subscribers it has. And, once the channel gets monetized, guess who gets a cut of the ad revenue collected? The youtuber of course! YouTube is a video distribution site, but ultimately its main goal is to get as many users as possible, in turn attracting massive human traffic, and for any platform that has loads of human traffic, it means that the platform itself is fertile ground for companies to market their products and services. This is how Ryan the kid youtuber made so much money. Of course, not all of his earnings was ad revenue, but I'm sure at some point in his YouTube career, it was. Do you think 22 million dollars paid out was a big sum for YouTube? I doubt so, they must have earned tons more from the companies who paid them to place ads in the first place! I'd highly recommend giving YouTube a try. Think of something that you enjoy doing. Fishing? Cooking? Playing games? Shopping? These are all pretty interest topics to build video content around. Let's say that you enjoy eating great food and you spend your weekends hunting for great eateries and restaurants. Instead of just simply eating, get a GoPro ready and do a video review on the dishes! You'd be surprised at how much fun it actually is making videos and posting them, especially if it is something that you have a passion for. Find your niche. Paired up with passion. You'll find yourself hooked to creating videos.

Of course, it is easier said than done, getting your YouTube channel monetized. There must be a lot of thought and time invested into the channel and video content, to really make it quality videos for viewers to enjoy. One critical factor to understand is the almighty YouTube algorithm, the system that decides if your video is worth being pushed to viewers. Search engine optimisation strategies must be implemented by the Youtuber as well, to help boost video searches.

Tons of work is required to build a successful channel, which is why the first question that you must answer for yourself is, that the niche that you decide to do videos about must be your passion. You have to enjoy doing it. If not, it will be chore for you to produce videos regularly.

Take your time with it. I'm not a YouTuber, but I sure am inspired by successful YouTubers and I follow a good number of them. One of my favourites is Graham Stephan. He is a real estate agent/ investor/ YouTuber, and his topics are always about money, investments, and personal finance. As of this year 2020, he has roughly 2.28 million subscribers. Back in 2019 he made a video about how much money he made on YouTube with 1 million subscribers, it was a whopping 1.2 million dollars. Now he is nowhere close to Ryan toysreview, but the reason why I enjoy his content so much is because he constantly brings his viewers back to when he first started putting videos on YouTube, how he started recording videos using just his iPhone, and how he grew his channel at a very gradual pace. He always said that he never did it for the money, but rather, he did it because he enjoyed sharing video content that he was passionate about. Lo and behold, this simple reason has led him to where his today in his YouTube standing. 2.28 million people tune in to listen to him rant about finance matters 3 times a week; think of all the ads that is constantly being flashed at his viewers, and the disgusting amounts of money that Mr Stephan is making, while he literally does nothing. Nothing at all.

Like most passive income strategies, it usually takes a huge amount of work, time, and energy to build the source of income before being able to actually see and enjoy the income. YouTubers can literally be pretty much hands off from the channel once it takes off (although most get even more motivated to produce more content). Mr Stephan did mention that he still makes ad revenue money from videos that he posted years ago, and that should he decide to stop making videos altogether, he would still be able to generate income from his older videos.

Affiliate marketing

Now, this ties in greatly with YouTube. So, let's say you start a YouTube channel reviewing audio equipment, and you managed to garner a good number of subscribers and you have a decent following. You can actually help these audio equipment companies with their marketing efforts, by doing a positive review for the equipment, and leaving a link or a discount code in your description. When people buy through your affiliate link, you get a small commission from the sale! A common affiliate programme to join is Amazon Associates; simply sign up for an account, choose the products that you would be reviewing, create an Amazon Affiliate link and presto! You are officially an affiliate.

Search engine optimisation

Let's talk a little about search engines. All big E commerce companies run on search engines; Google, yahoo, amazon, Alibaba etc. These search engines serve a fundamental need - to bring a relevant product/ service to a customer that is ready to purchase. This is why E commerce is so powerful. There is no more need for customers to physically hunt for any desired product. Just simply type in the search box and the search engine will find the item for you.

Rankings and keyword searches

With that in mind, how E commerce businesses make their money, is by first optimising their product search through rankings. E commerce businesses list their products online, inputting common keywords that people search for, and linking those keywords to their products. The search engine will then match the keyword relating to their product. The prospective buyer will click on their links, and they'll eventually be led to the product landing page where they can purchase the desired product or service.

Internet advertising

So, how does a company ensure that their website or product page is listed as the rank #1 in a search result? Well, they first need to make tons of sales to tell the search engine algorithm that the product is indeed relevant and saleable. Sounds like an tough fight right? Imagine a fresh company trying to compete with older companies with an E commerce presence? There's little or no chance that the new company can appear at rank #1 on the search result. This is where internet advertising comes in.

For instance, tech and E commerce giants Amazon and Google provide advertising services and charge users based on clicks. Let me explain how this works.

Impressions

Say a new company engages Amazon to market their products, what Amazon does is to put the company's product link in front of users as an advertisement. This is called an impression, since the user will see the advertisement. Amazon will only charge the company if the user clicks on the advertisement, whether or not the company buys the product is not Amazon's problem anymore; they have successfully directed customer traffic To the company's product page/ website. The rest of the work is up to the company's/ individual's ad copy (a sales letter that features the benefits of the product).

This is generally how internet advertising cost structure works; cost per click.

Ad copy

Now, this is like a product description, it applies to all E Commerce products and video distribution companies like YouTube (for YouTube, it's slightly different, content creators use thumbnails and compelling video titles to attract people to click on their links). It is like a product description, or a link description that compels a prospective customer to buy the product, or click on the link to watch the content in the video. Mastering ad copy is a powerful skill for individuals who want to succeed in online businesses.

E Commerce

Now this is interesting. Remember how when we wanted something in the past, we would need to go the physical store to actually buy our desired product? We go to a particular retail store, right? Not anymore. With the rise of E commerce, online retail stores are the new kids in town in the merchandising game. Blame it on Amazon and Alibaba. Or.. China, whichever way you want to spin this blame game.

Drop shipping

Think of how the old school supply chain management used to work. There are manufacturers, and retailers. The retailers would source products from the manufacturers, buy the goods wholesale, get a good discount for making a bulk purchase, store it in their warehouses and ship the goods out to all their retail outlets. The products would then be displayed in the retail storefront to entice customers to purchase their products. Now with E commerce, we can do away with the physical store presence. Why? Because human traffic has gone online! Furthermore, payment modes have become so much more convenient than say,10-15 years ago, there is really not much reason why customers should take the trouble to go out of their homes, into the malls and stores to buy products. They can simply go on a shopping spree from their own homes.

With this new culture, E commerce retail stores start to emerge; online retail stores that display items for sale via their websites. So now, wait a minute, Remember the whole supply chain process that was described earlier? Numerous agencies and tons of staff are required to work together to make the whole supply chain operation work. So then, how is one person going to run the whole supply chain operations? Won't the products need to be stored in warehouses; orders matched to customers addresses etc.? What about sourcing for manufacturers? Won't a whole team of merchandisers be required for that?

All valid questions, and all these questions can be solved, by engaging the services of an E commerce platform company.

Shopify

Shopify is an E commerce platform that helps online retailers set up an online store and sell their products. They provide a basic template your online store website, you can design it, beautify it, put useful instructional videos and tips on the products that you are selling. Shopify also handles all the warehousing, order tracking and even providing manufacturers and suppliers to its users. Shopify's business model is primarily a subscription service, so its users pay an annual fee to use all its resources and of course to get back end support as well.

Oberlo

Oberlo is a subsidiary of Shopify, and their main task is to facilitate the importing of products from retailers to customers, they handle all the logistics and warehousing. Best of all, the retailer bears no inventory risk! Back in the day, conventional retailers had to buy a ton of inventory to get a bulk discount, however, the risk was that the retailer would not know if he or she could sell all the product that was bought. In this day and age, with E commerce, the inventory is bought only when an order comes in. Oberlo handles this. They act as the middleperson linking manufacturers with retailers, who would then ultimately provide for the customers. Guess who their biggest supplier is? China! Or AliExpress. China is known as the world's factory because they can produce goods at a fraction of the costs of manufacturers in other parts of the world. Oberlo has direct links to AliExpress, if I'm not mistaken, all their products are from AliExpress. So, all the online retailer has to do is to source for customers! Drive traffic to their online retail store, or Shopify store. Products are so cheap that the retailer can mark up its retail price to 3 or 4 times its purchase cost!

The online retail business can be very lucrative, and the work involved is considerably less than conventional retail, and on top of that, everything can be done at home! Who knew that buying and selling products could be done in the comfort of your own home! By just one person!

Fulfilment by Amazon (FBA)

FBA is a similar E commerce business model. But, instead of having an online store, the sellers simply list their products in the Amazon universe. Amazon gives the retailer access to millions of customers.

So how exactly does FBA work, first, have a product to sell. Then, package the products according to the specifications that Amazon requires, and you simply send your prepared products to the Amazon fulfilment centres. These centres will settle the distribution to your buyers (the people who are buying your products through Amazon). Do take note that there are fulfilment fees and inventory storage fees involved in this particular business venture.

Self-published author

If you're someone who is knowledgeable about a topic, I would suggest that you get cracking on a book! Or an eBook. The book that you're reading now, took 7 days to get created. Best of all, it's free! You do not have to sink a ton of capital into inventory, or the physical publishing of the book itself, and finding a vendor to display your book. I'll get into the nitty gritty of publishing later. But first, let me share with you my story.

I have been obsessed with personal finance and the stock market since 2015. I devoured countless books on investments even till this day and will continue to be avid reader for the days to come. I just love reading so much. It expands my mind intellectually and psychologically as well. I constantly get inspired from these books. What better way to make a small impact to the world by penning down your knowledge into writing! From the time I started seriously reading, I probably read more than 200 books. My knowledge on investing became pretty extensive, and I soon found myself becoming the go to person in my workplace when it came to money, investments, and personal finance. It feels great to be known for a particular niche.

So one day, I finally decided to write a book. 3 months later, I published "The Retail Investor: How to Analyse Businesses in the Stock Market" on KDP.

So, what is KDP?

Kindle Direct Publishing (KDP)

Amazon developed an electronic reading device some time back called Kindle, and this device stores eBooks sold by Amazon. It's like the iPod (a device to store music tracks), but instead of storing music, the kindle stores eBooks that the user purchases. With kindle, you can download eBooks directly from the machine itself. Pretty cool.

Of course, with an eBook platform, amazon had to come up with a self-publishing service as well. Kindle direct publishing (KDP) was launched together with kindle in 2007. Now, indie authors can independently publish their books and sell them online via the kindle store.

Writing a book may seem like a daunting task. It can

be tiring, but it's not as difficult as you think. As always, you first need to be passionate about a subject. Then pen the chapter titles down so that you have a basic idea about what you would like to write with regards to that topic. Next, discipline yourself to write at least 500 to 1000 words at a certain time of the day. As you write, you'll get a momentum and snowball effect with your ideas. Before you know it, you'll be jotting down furiously because your typing speed can't keep up with your ideas! Trust me on this. Put it in a word document, format it nicely (just YouTube how to format an eBook) and upload your manuscript onto your KDP account. The initial set up is really easy and the instructions are simple to understand as well. Give it a try! You may already have material for a bestseller, you just don't know it yet.

So, how do authors earn money? Royalties of course! Once your book is in the Amazon market, the sky is the limit. Amazon makes payment so easy for users, and eBooks are significantly cheaper compared to physical books (price range is usually 2.99-9.99) so customers are more inclined to just buy the book to see what it's all about. As your book gains popularity (by purchases and reviews), the Amazon algorithm will feature your books even more to potential customers, and a virtuous cycle will take place, enabling you to earn even more book sales. And did I forget to mention, all this is complete passive? Initial work done is tough, but once your book is published, you can just sit back, relax, and let Amazon do the heavy lifting for you regarding marketing and promotion.

Another interesting feature of KDP is that once your book is published, KDP will automatically opt your book into KDP select. This special programme gets the book enrolled into Kindle unlimited, a book subscription service provided by Kindle. On top of the royalties that you get from book purchases, Amazon will also pay you per page read from the any user who borrows your book through kindle unlimited! How's that for awesome!? Ok, it's slightly less than half a cent per page. But if you gain more popularity and more readership, over time these pages can really add up. it's really meant to supplement your book sale royalties. You get income from online book purchases and pages read by borrowers. Let's get into a hypothetical situation. Say you wrote a book for 3.99 USD, and you get a book purchase every other day (remember that Amazon has hundreds of millions of users, so your book is potentially exposed to that amount of traffic), that's already almost 60 USD. Add on having 5 readers finish your book via kindle unlimited every day, that's another 60 USD (5 people x 100 pages x 30 days). That's a whole 120 USD every month, 1440 USD at the end of the year! And all this is being earned without you having to spend any more time on it, apart from the initial phase of writing and publishing the book.

I know, I make it sound like it's too good to be true. It's not impossible, but it's not easy as well, to get your book popular in Amazon. That's why further research is needed on how you can use better search optimisation strategies (similar to YouTube) so that your book will appear higher on the ranking page when users search for the topic that you wrote about. In addition, you need to hire a graphic designer to design a beautiful book cover for your book, and of course, write a compelling description for your book as well.

Publishing a great book and getting book sales off the ground is one asset that is so worth creating because the income generation at the end is just so passive.

Real estate

Now this is a big one. Real estate investing has been around for the longest time, and people make tons of money on buying and selling houses. More importantly, if you're going to venture into real estate for passive income, it would be wiser to focus on the steady rental income that it yields. This type of income is slightly different from the internet business though. A ton of capital is required for a real estate purchase, so you need to actually save up for a year or two before deciding to take the plunge. Of course you absolutely have to educate yourself on real estate investing! Pop by the library and devour any real estate book that you can find. Learn the ropes first. Don't blindly go to one open house and make a purchase on the spot. You are putting a lot of money at stake.

A reason why people get into real estate is that the property itself is tangible, and it solves a very essential need, shelter. Everybody needs a roof over their heads, and if you own a property, you can almost be certain that there will be a demand for it. The wealthiest people in the world own tons of properties. Donald Trump made his fortune in real estate. Robert Kiyosaki. Robert Kuok. Lee Ka-Shing. Barbara Corcoran. Grant Cardone, Mochtar Riady. These are all real estate moguls.

Another reason that real estate investing is so popular, is the leverage that it provides. Obviously, for the average middle-class worker, we will take many years to pay for a house fully in cash, we need to utilise debt to get into the game of real estate. Thankfully, banks are willing to lend money to make real estate purchases.

For any investor, the number one metric to determine if an investment is worthwhile is this, Return on Investment, or ROI. How much returns can I get, as the investor, off my initial capital outlay (principal) on a yearly basis? So, let's use a hypothetical scenario. Say you found an awesome apartment for $800,000, and the rental yield is $3,000 per month. This would make up an annual yield of 4.5% (12 months X $3,000 rental = $36,000, which makes up 4.5% of $800,000). Not too juicy right? If you were to save up $800,000 cash to purchase the apartment, that would be your yield. At 4.5%, you could have dollar cost averaged into an index ETF from day 1 of saving the $800k, and letting compound interest for you, rather than to save up for 5-7 years, letting the money sit in the back at less than 0.05% interest. The opportunity cost for saving the full payment of the apartment would be too much to bear. This is where the bank comes in. As a buyer, you can enlist the help of your bank to fund at least 80% of your purchase price, and you only need to come up with 20% as your capital outlay. Let's do some maths.

Purchase price of apartment: $800,000

Mortgage: 80% of $800,000 = $640,000

Your capital outlay: 20% of $800,000 = $160,000

See! With the help of a bank, you only need to come up with $160,000, a quarter of what you initially had to come up with. Now, this is where it gets juicy. Check it out.

Say the bank charges 3% interest on the mortgage, which makes up to an annual interest expense of $19,200 (3% X $640k X 12 months). We also know that we can yield $24,000 annually from rental income.

Annual rental income = $36,000

Annual interest expense = $19,200

Annual cashflow from apartment = $36,000 - $19,200 = $16,800.

Now, this $16,800 cashflow is your ROI. What is $16.8k of $160k? That is a 10.5% cash on cash return! This phenomenon is called leverage in the finance world. People get into real estate because of leverage.

Before you dis my simplistic example, yes there are other factors and expenses that come into play here, like maintenance costs, advertising for tenants etc. The point that I'm trying to get across is that with real estate, you can really get a boost in your returns as you have an ally to help you, the bank. At 10.5% return, you can double your money in less than 7 years. Amazing right?

Real estate is the bomb. It's one of the most exciting ways to build wealth. Relating back to our financial security numbers, calculate how much capital you would actually need to hit the target. Say you have learnt the ways of real estate and you are experienced enough to get great real estate deals that yield 10.5% cash every year. If your total yearly expenses is $24,000, you technically only need less than $230,000 to be financially secure! How's that for an "alternative" source of income?

Let's talk a little bit about the capital appreciation part. If the apartment were to increase its value by $800,000, the new price of the apartment would be $880,000. Let's see how much money the investor makes from the sale.

Cash received from sale of apartment: $880,000

Return the loan: $640,000

Residual cash: $880,000-$640,000 = $240,000

Initial capital outlay: $160,000

Capital appreciation: $(240,000-160,000)/160,000 = a whopping 50% increase in capital appreciation!!

See the power of leverage? You only needed the apartment to increase its value by 10% to get an actual 50% cash on cash capital appreciation, on top of the years of collecting a 10.5% annual rental yield. An obscene amount of money can potentially be made in real estate.

A word of caution: never over-lever. Debt is double edged sword, if you use it wisely you can augment your overall returns, if you use excessively, it will complete decimate your wealth. Always consider the fact that there will be times that tenants are hard to find, and that your property may be vacant, while still having the obligation to pay the mortgage expense. Don't let your real estate by the banks.

Part time work for special services

What do you do on the weekends? Anything productive? Chances are, you would be partying with friends, getting wasted and watching Netflix. Why not do something useful? When I was in my teenage years, I was fortunate enough to use my other skills to earn income. I was a music teacher, and I got paid $20 an hour to teach music to young kids. I worked on Friday evenings and the whole of Saturday. Bear in mind that I was around 18-19 years old back then. I was pulling an average of $600 per month! Not too shabby for an alcoholic teen, right? Unfortunately, I was too dumb back then to save, and I blew it all on parties and liquor. What I'm trying to say here is, when you have spare time on your hands, make it a point to spend some of your free hours working part time! There must be another skill that you're good at! Do a cooking class, be a swimming coach. Personal trainer. I see a lot of people in great shape, but I doubt they do any private training. Give private maths tuition to struggling youngsters. Do something that can earn you some extra income. Remember, capitalise on your youth to work your tail off, so that when you get older, you can reap the fruits of your labour. Imagine your freedom fund starting off as a seedling, and you water it, nourish, in time it will grow into a tree, and you can bask in its shade.

CHAPTER 8

Generosity.

C ongratulations on reaching the end of this book. With the knowledge you have now, I'm certain that you would be able to achieve financial freedom in the years to come. Let's explore the choices you can have once you have financial freedom.

Settling essential expenses easily

With the passive income that you have, you do not have to worry for another day in your life that you won't be able to afford water, electricity, and food. It's all taken care of by your freedom fund.

Entertainment is almost unlimited

If you choose to work even after achieving financial freedom, you will have tons more liquidity to do the things that you enjoy. It's almost to a point where, you can recklessly spend your money on a short holiday every month, and not even make a dent on your salary.

You wouldn't even need to use your earned income. Imagine that. Or, if you have that dream car that you always wanted to buy, you can simply save the income that comes from your freedom fund and make the purchase with those savings. It would look a little strange though, if say you were a simple schoolteacher and you own a Jaguar (people might think you peddle heroine on the side, sorry for bad joke, I kid).

Setting aside funds for kids college

For those of you capitalist pigs with piglets to support, your freedom fund can buy your kids a good education. Don't tell them that though, you don't want them to take their privileges for granted.

Helping family with health issues

Healthcare costs are constantly rising. Wouldn't it be a relief to be able to pick up the bill for an ailing family member? Or even for yourself (touch wood), if you get sick, of course you have insurance, but it wouldn't be better to have more buffer funds so that you do not have to sell your own personal assets. Your freedom fund can give you a peace of mind when health troubles start to come your way.

Insurance for the single breadwinner

To add to my previous point, say a household has a single breadwinner and the breadwinner gets sick, and is unable to work. If the family had a freedom fund in place, at least the income generated from the freedom fund can replace the breadwinner's income, in turn maintaining the standard of living for the whole family.

I've mentioned a lot about what your freedom fund can do for you. But remember, God did not allow you to have wealth just to fund your luxurious lifestyle. You will never truly be a champion of money if you do not utilise it to help your fellow men. If you hoard all the money you've earned for yourself, chances are, you'll never be able to experience the single greatest joy that anyone can feel, the joy of giving, being outrageously generous. And why? Why is it so counter intuitive that the greatest joy in the world is giving? Because when you give, you subconsciously show yourself and your brain that you don't live in a world of scarcity anymore, you live in a world of abundance, and when you feel the sense of abundance in your life, you'll never be slave to the feeling of lack any more. That's when you know you have truly attained the status of a money champion. God bless!

FINAL WORD

Money is sacred, don't let anyone tell you different. Don't be fooled by the saying that money is the root of all evil. It's not. It's the "love" of money, that is the root of all evil. People kill for money, people steal for money, why? Because they simply do not have it, and they become desperate because they can't support themselves and their families. Frankly, what I firmly believe in is, the lack of money is the root of all evil. I say this many times, ignorance is not bliss, ignorance is poverty, and I hate poverty, you should too. Sorry, let me rephrase. I HATE THE POVERTY MINDSET. Why? Because poverty leads to ruination and perdition. Poverty kills societies. Women and children are battered, and men resort to crime. Bad things happen to poverty-stricken neighbourhoods. It makes me sad to see people with narrow-minded, blocked mindsets about life and wealth, that they drive themselves towards poverty eventually, or at least, they work for 40 years of their lives and have nothing much to show for it at the end. Look, I'm not saying that I hate poor people, let me just put it out there. There are countries and peoples who are politically oppressed, hungry and without opportunity. They were unfortunately born in a place where they simply cannot get ahead and have no choice but to endure a harsh life. I get that. Don't you think that all the more we should find ways to help them? Wouldn't our purpose on earth be more meaningful then? The bulk of us who are probably reading this book would belong to the more fortunate bunch of people who have had good education, adequate food to eat and a roof over our heads. Chances are that people like us belong to the richest countries in the world. And yet, we take things for granted. Most of us have no goal, no vision, no discipline, and we mindlessly fill our homes and hearts with useless and meaningless material things. We "need" new clothes, we "need" to eat a steak dinner every night, we "need" Netflix. Ugh, this makes the Big Jodhi sick. Have some perspective please. We constantly take for granted the good things in life, and we squander our hard-earned money, while other people are so dirt poor they can't even afford to eat. It's time to have a change in our thinking and make the best out of the time we have on this earth.

Big Jodhi

ABOUT THE AUTHOR

Big Jodhi

Big Jodhi is just an Average Joe who loves reading about money and thinking about money in his spare time. He loves stories about capitalism and his heroes include Cornelius Vanderbilt, JP Morgan, Jay Gould, Benjamin Graham, John Templeton, Warren Buffet, Peter Lynch, Walter Schloss, Seth Klarman, Mohnish Pabrai, Kevin O'Leary, Howard Marks,  Lee Ka-Shing, Robert Kuok, Mochtar Riady and Joel Greenblatt.

BOOKS BY THIS AUTHOR

The Retail Investor: How To Analyze Businesses And Invest Your Money Like A Pro In The Stock Market

This book will give you an insight on the basics of the stock market investing. It contains all the info you need to invest safely and wisely! Grab a copy now!

The Retail Investor: How To Analyze Reits And Invest Your Money Like A Pro In The Stock Market

This book teaches you how to the basics of Real Estate Investment Trusts, what it is, how it works and how you can build passive income for yourself using this wonderful investment vehicle! Grab a copy now!

The Retail Investor 3 Books In 1: Invest Masterfully And Achieve Financial

Freedom

This book combines all 3 volumes of The Retail Investor series. Why buy the individual books when you can have all 3 in 1 book! At a cheaper price too! Grab a copy now!

www.ingramcontent.com/pod-product-compliance
Lightning Source LLC
Chambersburg PA
CBHW020620220526
45463CB00006B/2638